Outlines

Improvised Group Drama

for 14-year-olds and over

S. G. Nash M.A.

Schofield & Sims Ltd. Huddersfield

Printed in England by David Green Printers Ltd.
Kettering, Northants

Contents

How to use this book

The material is intended to encourage role-playing within the dynamics of group activity. The outlines (or skeletons for improvised plays) are graded and designed to emphasise different aspects of dramatic technique. Each outline is followed by topics for discussion and written work which, it is hoped, will add interest besides consolidating the work of the teacher.

The following is the suggested procedure for using the book but this can easily be varied to suit the individual teacher. Details of plot and characterisation can also be varied under the teacher's guidance.

It should be possible to work through one outline in a double period.

1 The class should divide into groups of five or six. The group elects a producer, who is then responsible for the work of that group.

2 The group should spend ten minutes on one, or more, of the **Preliminary exercises**. Care should be taken not to spend too much time on this section.

Alternatively, the teacher may wish to undertake these exercises with the whole class before the division into groups.

3 During the next ten minutes the group should study the **Your play** section, allocate parts, and closely consider the **Characterisation** and the **Particular points to rehearse**.

4 The next fifteen minutes should be spent in rehearsing the first part of the play.

The group should then consider how to continue and end their improvisation—this should take a further ten minutes and is the time when the teacher's assistance is usually called for!

5 Some forty-five minutes after the start of the lesson the groups should now be able to act their work, watched by the class.

This should then leave time for the **Topics for discussion** in the remaining ten minutes of a seventy minute lesson. The **Supplementary exercises** could also be used at this point.

Most schools timetable Drama in double periods; if not, or if the session is an out-of-school one, the activity could be split into two halves.

Outline 1   The Great Fire

Preliminary exercises

Conditions of great heat are uncomfortable. Mime the discomfort of explorers in a hot desert or sultry jungle, scientists near the brim of a volcano, or steelworkers toiling near a furnace.

A fire is discovered—perhaps in an enclosed caravan or whilst enjoying a picnic in a forest. Show people's various reactions.

Imagine a room filled with choking fumes and heat. Dramatise your escape.

Characterisation

Will
Industrious and cheerful. Enjoys his work and treats customers with courtesy and respect.

Anne
Will's capable wife. Middle-aged, jolly and rather plump from helping herself to the food which she prepares!

Mary
Young, attractive daughter of Will and Anne. She dislikes hard work and is secretly fond of the idle apprentice, Dirk. Nevertheless she does her best to please her parents and their customers.

Dirk
Lazy, clumsy and a little stupid.

Miss Martha
Rich, haughty, upper-class spinster who hates shopping.

Your play

Will	the baker
Anne	Will's wife
Mary	their daughter
Dirk	an apprentice
Miss Martha	an awkward customer

Scene   Pudding Lane Bakery, London in 1666 (The Great Fire of London started at a bakery in Pudding Lane. It extended rapidly in the strong winds and destroyed almost the whole of the centre of the city.)

Here is an outline of how your play should start—it is up to you to show how it should finish. Make sure you agree how the scene is set—where the ovens, the door and so forth are.

1   Will and Anne are in the hot bakery preparing bread for the ovens. (Anne kneads dough, Will shapes the loaves and puts them into ovens.)

2   Will calls for help from *Dirk* who *enters* lazily. Will orders him to fetch more wood for the ovens and *Dirk* sullenly *exits*.

3   *Miss Martha*, a wealthy and awkward customer, *enters* to purchase several items. She is a fussy person and keeps changing her mind as *Mary enters* to serve her.

4   *Dirk* re-*enters* with the wood and carelessly starts to stoke the ovens. Anne stops her work and crosses to Mary to assist her in serving the irritable Miss Martha.

5   Eventually Miss Martha completes her purchases and Dirk comes over to help her carry her goods out into the street. *Miss Martha and Dirk exeunt.*

6   *Dirk* rapidly re-*enters* shouting that Miss Martha has slipped in the mud and fallen into a street gutter, injuring her ankle.

7   *Will* hastily *exits* and soon re-*enters* half carrying the injured *Miss Martha*.

8   Mary and Anne come to assist Miss Martha to a chair whilst Dirk returns to stoking the ovens. *Will exits*—for a glass of ale!

9   Suddenly Mary smells burning . . .

What happens next? How did the Great Fire begin? Decide at what point you will finish your play.

Particular points to rehearse

a   In order to create the busy atmosphere of a shop, people must be constantly entering and departing. Practise this and contrast all the activity with Dirk's idleness. What do characters who remain 'on-stage' say whilst people are making entrances and exits?

b   Several things occur on stage simultaneously; e.g. Dirk stokes the oven whilst Anne and Mary serve Martha (what is Will doing?). In rehearsal always ensure that positioning is clear and decide which is the most important activity—in this case the serving of the customer.

Will
Practise the strenuous and hot work of preparing loaves for the oven.
Your dislike of Dirk's laziness must be made obvious. How will you portray this—as well as showing the jollier side to your character?

Anne
Practise your mime for kneading dough. Show what hot, hard work it is.
Rehearse the way in which you assist in serving the angry Martha; also think about how you will treat her when she injures her ankle.

Mary
Rehearse the sequence where you serve Martha, offering different goods. Is this meant to be a comic episode?

Dirk
Consider how best to portray a clumsy and lazy character. Are you trying to appear comic or as rather sad?
Prepare the mime for the heavy work of stoking fires, carrying wood, assisting with the cumbersome purchases of Miss Martha.

Miss Martha
How will you portray a haughty, distasteful character?
Rehearse your indignation at having to go shopping, also the overacted pain—and damage to your dignity—suffered by your fall into the gutter!

EVERYONE
How will your character react to the fire?

Topics for discussion after a group's performance

◉ Could the group improvise another scene about a fire, perhaps from a different point of view (e.g. firemen called out on a false alarm)?

◉ Choose two individuals to act an episode between a shop assistant and an awkward customer, then have them swap roles and repeat the episode.

◉ Could the play have been presented in mime only? If so, what differences of approach are required to make the plot obvious to the audience?

◉ How convincingly did the characters react to the discovery of the fire? Comment on the way in which the group brought their play to its conclusion.

◉ Elaborate on Mary's feelings towards Dirk as presented by the group. How convincing were the other relationships between characters portrayed? Did some overplay their parts by appearing too comic or as caricatures?

◉ Consider how Miss Martha might be portrayed in a different setting, such as a contemporary scene at a Garden Party or School Prize Day.

◉ Suggest some historical research that you would like to do on the Great Fire. Besides the Great Fire itself, you could investigate the role of an apprentice, money and the cost of goods, the sort of food eaten, pictures of old London or the contribution to London architecture of Sir Christopher Wren.

Topics for written work

◉ Write a short piece of dialogue between a shop assistant and an awkward customer, clearly bringing out the characters of both.

◉ Write a newspaper report on the Great Fire as though you had been there to witness it.

◉ Write a short, vivid description—or poem—about a fire.

◉ Write a helpful criticism of one group's performance of THE GREAT FIRE, giving suggestions for improvements as well as praising good features.

Outline 2   Night In The Waxworks

Preliminary exercises

Mime some physical activity (e.g. decorating a wall, erecting a tent, serving a meal) and at a given signal freeze, statue-like, and stand motionless.

Rehearse the jerky movements of puppets, robots and waxwork models. Show them 'coming to life' in awkward, stiff actions.

Characterisation

Anthea
Age about 14, timid and shy, but with a quiet sense of humour. Sensible and resourceful.

Paul
Age about 15, mischievous and rather a 'show-off'; he conceals his fears with an outward show of bravery and high spirits.

Mr Dane
Elderly, simple-minded and rather slow. He is continually chuckling to himself and knows all about the waxworks' secret.

Dr Scull
The waxwork model of some evil murderer. What details can be added to this character?

Monster from Mars
Let your imagination run riot to improvise this horrific fiend from outer space. Are there any 'props' or articles of clothing with which to disguise your appearance? Think how you will move, and the sort of sounds you will make.

Your play

Anthea } Paul }	children
Mr Dane	the attendant
Dr Scull } Monster from Mars }	waxwork models

Scene   the Chamber of Horrors

One of the hardest things to do on stage is simply to stand still. See how you can handle this situation!

1. On stage are the waxwork models of the horrific Dr Scull and the Monster from Mars, frozen in threatening and terrifying positions.

2. Two children, *Paul* and *Anthea, enter* the Chamber of Horrors and curiously examine the models. They laugh and pull faces at the motionless figures.

3. *Mr Dane,* the attendant, shouts from *off-stage* that he is locking up and that all visitors must leave. Giggling, Paul and Anthea stand in grotesque postures with the waxworks and pretend to be models as well, remaining absolutely motionless as *Mr Dane enters*.

4. *Mr Dane,* a rather simple sort of person, believes that the children are new additions to the collection. He scrutinises them, dusts them down and *exits*, locking the door.

5. Paul and Anthea return to life, laughing at their joke. They try to leave and discover that the door is locked! Anthea is frightened and Paul tries to comfort her.

6. Suddenly Anthea screams and swears that the waxwork models have moved! (In fact they do move slightly, and then 'freeze' again into new postures when the children turn to look at them.)

7. Slowly, the waxwork models come stiffly to life and move menacingly towards the children . . .

What will happen next? How will your play end?

Particular points to rehearse

a   Contrast the laughter and light-heartedness at the opening of your play with the horror and panic which develops.

b   Prepare carefully the timing for Mr Dane's entry, and the movements of the models as they 'come to life'.

c   Discuss how you might build up the suspense as the play proceeds.

Anthea
Demonstrate carefully the contrast in your moods, from curiosity and light-heartedness to horror and panic. Build up the suspense by building up your fear and terror.

Paul
Consider carefully the display of your emotions. At what points will you let your fear show, and at what times will you conceal it with a display of mock-bravery and joking?

Mr Dane
Prepare your character study of an elderly person: the slow walk, bent back, hunched shoulders, stiffening joints and creaking voice. What do you know about the secret of the waxworks? Consider the timing of your first entry, allowing the children time to join the models.

Dr Scull and Monster from Mars
Prepare carefully the timing of your movements when you first start to 'come to life'. Rehearse the stiff, menacing movements of these horrific waxworks. Think how the play might end.

EVERYONE
Although the first part of the play may be amusing, do not let your faces slip; and remember that the second half of the play must be horrific and frightening without being overacted.

Topics for discussion after a group's performance

● How difficult was it to move from the humour of the opening into the horror of the second half? Was the group successful or did it overact? Was there a gradual build up of suspense? If not, how might this have been achieved?

● What particular lighting and sound effects could be used if they were available?

● How successful was Anthea in varying her mood and building up her horrified reactions? How clearly did Paul portray the conflict of his emotions between mock-bravery and fear?

● How successful was Mr Dane's part in the play? What difficulties were encountered in acting the part of an elderly person and how were they overcome? How would Mr Dane appear in another setting, such as seated on a park bench? Would he appear sinister?

● Was there a contrast in the acting between the youthful characters (Paul and Anthea) and the elderly Mr Dane?

● The techniques of standing motionless concern problems of anticipation and balance. How well did the group cope with these?

● Suggest other situations, not necessarily horrific, in a play where statues or puppets might come to life.

● Hold a class discussion on horror stories. Which book or horror film have you found particularly frightening? What was it in the treatment that made the film so effective?

Topics for written work

● Write a short story in which statues, puppets, or toys come to life.

● Mr Dane writes a letter to the local newspaper complaining about the behaviour of young people today. Write this letter.

● Write a review of a book or film which you thought was a good horror story. Why do you think people like this kind of story? Suggest some reasons in your review.

● Design a costume for the Monster from Mars in your group's play.

Outline 3　　　Cave In!

Preliminary exercises

Vividly mime movements to show your progress through a narrow underground cave or pot-hole; e.g. squeeze through tunnels, balance on ledges, wade through water, struggle through darkness.

Two parties are separated in a cave by a minor rock fall. Show how the two groups communicate through this imaginary obstacle.

Each actor imagines himself enclosed in a large transparent box. He pushes against the 'walls' attempting, hopelessly, to escape from his claustrophobic prison.

Characterisation

Dennis
An experienced pot-holer and climber, leader of the party. Brave and resourceful, but sometimes over excited.

Trevor
Impetuous and inconsiderate. Easily frightened and rather cowardly.

Jack
Quiet, clever, considerate.

Liz
Emotional and excitable but with hidden strength of character.

Carol
Calm and reserved on the surface, but panics easily.

Your play

Dennis
Trevor
Jack　　　young pot-holers
Liz
Carol

Scene　a claustrophobic pot-hole
The story is a simple one about some young people who go pot-holing (exploring narrow underground passages and caves) and become trapped.
The quality of your production will depend on how well the actors depict their movements underground: squeezing through crevices, edging along a ledge, wading through icy water, scaling obstacles and so on. You must pay particular attention to movement and 'map a route' across the whole extent of your acting area.

1　*All* five pot-holers *enter* the underground passage through a narrow pot-hole.
They squeeze forward along the passage (following the route which you have planned).

2　Eventually, Trevor excitedly discovers what appear to be some cave-paintings and the others examine them. Trevor decides to move on, but the girls are becoming rather frightened and only reluctantly agree.

3　Dennis decides to return to the surface to fetch a camera to photograph the cave-paintings. He arranges with Jack to leave marks on the walls so that he can follow them when he returns. He now crawls back to the entrance.

4　Suddenly a cave-in separates the two parties! (The way you depict this catastrophe is important: the looks of fear, the panic, the vain attempts to escape and the way in which the pot-holers comfort one another.)

5　Trevor's party is entombed. Dennis has anxiously retraced his steps to discover a solid wall of rock between himself and his friends . . .

What happens next?

Particular points to rehearse

a Plan the underground route carefully over the acting area and maintain the atmosphere of moving underground throughout your performance.

b Contrast the excitement of discovering the cave-paintings with the horror and subsequent panic of the cave-in.

Dennis
Establish yourself as leader of the party and decide how you will organise the route.
Prepare your reaction to the rock fall as well as to the discovery of the cave-paintings. Will you blame yourself for leaving the party to fetch the camera?

Trevor
What incidents will demonstrate your impetuosity and lack of consideration for others?
Prepare your excited discovery of the cave-paintings, and your fear at being trapped underground.

Jack
Rehearse your reaction to the cave-in and your subsequent behaviour. What incidents can you devise to show your strength of character? Could you help the others to escape?
Consider how, and where, you will leave marks for Dennis to follow.

Liz
Think about your character's emotional and excited reactions to everything—particularly the cave-paintings and the rock fall.
Consider how you will help Jack reorganise and encourage the party, particularly Carol.

Carol
Contrast your early aloofness with your later hysteria and panic. Rehearse this difficult portrayal of hysteria and think what incident could bring you back to your senses.

EVERYONE
Two factors will affect the success of your play. Firstly, the representation of movement underground; and secondly, the interesting and varied characters of the people involved.

Topics for discussion after a group's performance

- How successful was the actors' portrayal of movement underground? Was the route varied and interesting?

- Was there sufficient contrast between the opening and closing scenes of the play?

- How well did the actors depict the contrasting personalities of the characters? Did any character appear to show several sides to his or her nature? Were their interactions convincing?

- How would these same characters behave in a different setting such as a discotheque or party? Who would emerge as the natural leader?

- What other plays might be set in a cave? The group could contrast the daily activities of a Stone Age family with that of a twentieth-century family who come to visit that same cave.

- In this play the acting area was mapped out to represent a geographical route. How could this technique be employed in other plays?

Topics for written work

- Write a short adventure story about a group of children lost in a forest, or in a cave, or on moorland.

- Write two character studies—one of a cowardly person and one of a brave person.

- Write a story about some twentieth-century tourists transported back in time whilst visiting a Stone Age cave.

- Draw a plan of your acting area, and then map out on it the route which your group should ideally use in your play about the cave-in.

Preliminary exercises

A bomb must be defused! Individuals from your group mime this delicate operation.

Mime the movements of a diver getting into his wet suit, face-mask and breathing apparatus. Now put on your flippers and try walking around!

Characterisation

Captain Rufus
Resolute, calm and authoritative.

Lieutenant Commander Carol Cooper
Nervous, excitable first officer.

Lieutenant Harris
Resourceful, brave, very experienced.

Petty Officer Spender
A skilful engineer with a disregard for danger—and authority.

Dr Emma Bailey
Eccentric, brilliant scientist; she adores nuclear physics and could not bear to see the mine destroyed.

Your play

Captain Rufus	Submarine Captain
Lt. Cdr. Carol Cooper	Navigator
Lieutenant Harris	Communications Officer
Petty Officer Spender	Engineer
Dr Emma Bailey	Scientist

Scene   aboard a submarine

1 Rufus, Cooper and Harris are on stage aboard a submarine. (What are their tasks?) Captain Rufus explains to the others that their mission is to locate, capture, and disarm one of the enemy's new underwater nuclear mines.

2 Harris, operating a special sonic device, excitedly locates one of the mines. Rufus orders Cooper to set an appropriate course, and calls for Dr Emma Bailey.

3 *Emma Bailey*, the scientist, *enters* and explains to the captain about the mine and how best to capture it. A diver is required and Harris bravely volunteers.

4 Harris puts on diving equipment whilst Rufus issues orders. *Harris exits* through an air lock. (How will you portray this?)

5 Rufus, Cooper and Bailey wait anxiously and provide a commentary on what Harris is doing. *Spender* is called for and *enters*. Rufus explains the situation to him and adds that it will be Spender's task to disarm the mine.

6 *Harris re-enters* carrying a small packet—the nuclear mine! Rufus congratulates Harris as Spender and Bailey examine the bomb.

7 The mine must be disarmed. Spender carefully begins the removal of the fuse. Bailey discovers that the mine contains four different fuse mechanisms!

8 Cooper moves closer to examine the mine. Accidentally she nudges Spender's arm. Spender exclaims that the mine has started to tick!

9 Bailey confirms that one of the time fuses has been activated and that the device will explode in exactly ninety seconds . . .

What happens in these remaining seconds? How will your play end?

Particular points to rehearse

a Maintain throughout the impression of working within the close confines of a submarine.

b Practise and discuss how to portray the breath-taking suspense of defusing the mine. Consider how the different characters will react and how your play will end.

Rufus
Portray strongly the authority of your character and consider the sort of commands you will give. Think about your attitude towards the different members of your crew.

Cooper
Think of the moments where stress or excitement occur in the play and how you will react.

Harris
Practise your representation of a diver. Think how you will exit from the submarine. Does the audience see you 'swim' away or can you devise a more subtle exit?

Spender
What incidents would convey the unconventional nature of your character?
Rehearse the delicate defusing of the mine. Be careful not to make your movements too 'fussy' as the audience must follow what is happening.

Bailey
Devise some scientific knowledge of the mine and think how you will display your eccentric concern for its safety, showing a foolish disregard for danger.

EVERYONE
How will you react to the final crisis?
How should the play end?

Topics for discussion after a group's performance

◉ How convincingly did the characters react to the stress of their situation? How were the different reactions to the captain's authority portrayed?

◉ How successful was the group's portrayal of a submarine interior? Was Harris's depiction of a diver convincing? Is it possible, or desirable, to show him 'swimming'?

◉ What were the important aspects of the story? How well were these portrayed? When the mine was being defused how did the audience react? Were they held by the suspense? Did this incident trigger off strong reactions from the actors? If so, did anyone reveal something new about his or her character?

◉ How successful was the group's conclusion to the play? If the mine had exploded (and perhaps it did), how could this be portrayed on stage? Would it have been effective to 'freeze' the action just in the last seconds, leaving the audience in suspense?

◉ The group could try to imagine how their characters would recall the incident when safely on shore, perhaps with their friends in a pub.

◉ Discuss other improvisations which work towards a situation of stress; e.g. a plane hi-jack, the experience of hostages, a teacher with a naughty class.

Topics for written work

◉ Write a short story about one of the situations of stress discussed at the end of the previous section.

◉ Write a review of an adventure programme seen recently on television.
Select a scene, or incident, and say why it was particularly exciting.

◉ Write one half of a dialogue spoken into a telephone, from which we may gather what the whole conversation is about.

◉ Write about your group's production of DANGEROUS MISSION, saying what problems were encountered and how you tried to overcome them.

Outline 5

Blind Cyclops

Preliminary exercises

Consider in mime and by discussion how you would enter the mouth of a dark, unexplored cave.

Mime the heavy and ponderous movements of a giant, using large, exaggerated gestures. Discuss how the one-eyed Cyclops in your play could be portrayed.

Characterisation

Odysseus (Odd-ee-see-us)
A legendary Greek warrior; returning to his homeland, Ithaca, after many adventures following the fall of Troy. Strong, courageous and clever. A mighty leader of men.

Eurylochus (Yew-rill-o-cus)
Proud, powerful, loyal. Superstitious, believes he and his companions are under a curse.

Helen
A timid and beautiful princess.

Thea
Young, ferocious, tough female; enjoys adventure. Scornful of Helen.

Polyphemus the Cyclops (Poll-ee-fee-mus Sigh-clops)
A one-eyed giant. Loves devouring human flesh! Horrific and rather stupid.

Your play

Odysseus	Greek warrior king
Eurylochus	a proud Greek warrior
Helen	a timid princess
Thea	a young warrior maiden
Polyphemus	the Cyclops, a one-eyed giant

Scene   inside the giant's cave

1 *Odysseus* and his three comrades—*Eurylochus, Helen* and *Thea*—cautiously *enter* the Cyclops' mysterious, gloomy cave. Inside they light a fire and discover some cheese and a slaughtered lamb to eat.

2 Suddenly the horrific *Cyclops enters*. He discovers the terrified intruders and rolls a huge boulder in front of the cave's mouth to prevent their escape. He then informs his captives that he intends to devour them the next morning for his breakfast!

3 Odysseus attempts to calm his frightened colleagues and puts his plan for escape into action. Firstly, he greets the Cyclops and, in a friendly manner, offers him wine.

4 Polyphemus—the Cyclops—drinks the wine and demands more. Odysseus and his colleagues keep supplying wine until the giant falls asleep, drunk!

5 Eurylochus discovers a stake of wood and sharpens it to a point with his sword. Thea assists him whilst the terrified Helen hides.

6 Odysseus hardens the pointed stake by thrusting it into the fire. He then orders Thea and Helen to take the hot, pointed stake and thrust it into the Cyclops' single eye as he sleeps.

7 Blinded and enraged the Cyclops awakes in a fury. Now is the chance for Odysseus and his band to escape . . .

But how are they to get the giant to remove the boulder from the mouth of the cave?

Particular points to rehearse

a   Several interesting mimes are involved: the cooking of food, the Cyclops rolling the boulder, preparing the fire, sharpening the wooden stake, blinding the giant. Practise these.

b   Rehearse the giant's movements and voice; remember that he is not a comic character. Practise the general reaction to his arrival on the scene. Contrast this with the previous atmosphere of warmth and light offered by the fire on which food is being eagerly prepared.

Odysseus
Consider the sequence where you get the giant drunk. Think how you will portray a pretence of friendliness towards him.
Remember that you are a legendary leader. How will you establish your character early in the action?

Eurylochus
Prepare your mime for lighting a fire; also your sharpening of a large, imaginary stake of wood.

Helen
Contrast your timid behaviour with Thea's bravery; practise with her the way in which you will blind the Cyclops—showing considerable anxiety and reluctance. Could you try to persuade Eurylochus to do this instead of you?

Thea
Clearly portray your fearless nature and your scorn for Helen.
Rehearse the blinding of the Cyclops with her.

Polyphemus
Maintain the horror of your lumbering, stupid giant and prepare a dramatic entry. Prepare your pain and fury when you are blinded. Rehearse the sequence where you fall into a drunken stupor, but be careful never to make your character appear comic.

EVERYONE
Think how the play might end. How will you trick the giant into removing the boulder from the cave's entrance?

Topics for discussion after a group's performance

◉ How ingenious was the ending of the play? Does anyone in the class know how the warriors tricked the Cyclops in the original of Homer's 'Odyssey'?

◉ How successful were the several mimes in the play? Suggest activities for further mime involving weapons or the movement of heavy objects.

◉ How well did the actors establish the nature of their characters? How much background detail is required for this play? Was there a convincing contrast between Helen and Thea? How would these girls behave in a modern setting?

◉ How convincingly did Polyphemus portray his part? Did it become comic when it should not have done? How dramatic was his first entry? How convincing was the drinking sequence? Was the final pain and fury realistic?

◉ Discuss how a director might stage the play. What scenery would he use? How would one use make-up to create a Cyclops? What lighting would be used? Can you suggest suitable background music to create atmosphere?

◉ Some of the details of this legend (blinding, flesh-eating) are rather gory. Hold a discussion on these aspects of theatre.

◉ Discuss other legends which might be suitable for a short play. The school library and your local public library should have plenty of source material on such stories.

Topics for written work

◉ Draw a picture of the Cyclops; then write a vivid description or poem about him.

◉ Write a list of stage-properties necessary for a production of your group's play about the Cyclops, assuming that whatever you want is available.

◉ Write a short essay stating your views about violence in the theatre or on television.

◉ Design an exciting stage-set for a production of BLIND CYCLOPS.

Outline 6 — The Invisible Man

Preliminary exercises

When performing this play you must imagine that there is an invisible person involved. Each actor must be sure where this invisible person is located at each stage of the play so that they can react suitably to an unseen 'presence'.

Although he cannot be seen, he can be felt; e.g. sitting in an apparently empty chair, tripping over him, bumping into him, being hit by him, and so on.

Rehearse some incidents of this type.

Characterisation

Dr Wells
Elderly, eccentric, absent-minded scientist with an impish sense of humour. He dislikes Mr Pill, enjoys teasing Mrs Green, and is fond of practical jokes.

Rosemary
Attractive and good humoured.

Stuart
Fond of Rosemary but rather shy and bashful.

Mrs Green
A good-natured charlady; she is easily amused—and easily frightened.

Mr Pill
A rather sour and bitter business man; he has no sense of humour.

Your play

Dr Wells	?
Rosemary	Dr Wells's assistant
Stuart	Rosemary's friend
Mrs Green	a cleaning lady
Mr Pill	a chemist

Scene   inside a laboratory

1 *Rosemary* and *Stuart enter* the laboratory. Rosemary explains that Dr Wells has been trying out some new experiments and has not been seen for some days. Stuart is inspecting the apparatus when Rosemary suddenly laughs helplessly as she is tickled by some invisible presence! Naturally, she accuses Stuart who reacts indignantly.

2 *Mrs Green,* the cleaning lady, *enters* and explains that she has come to tidy the laboratory. Stuart asks her about Dr Wells. During the conversation Rosemary appears to be tickled again! Whilst she accuses Stuart of doing this, Mrs Green cries out in horror—she claims to keep bumping into something invisible and finally her duster is snatched from her hand by some unseen force. (How will she mime this, using a handkerchief?)

3 At this point *Mr Pill enters* and angrily demands to see Dr Wells, who owes him money for several chemist's bills. Rosemary attempts to explain his absence and examines the bills. Bitterly, Mr Pill says what he thinks of Dr Wells when he is suddenly hit on the head by some invisible force!

4 Events now reach their climax. Mrs Green is tripped up, Rosemary is tickled until she is hysterical with laughter, Stuart's hair is pulled and Mr Pill is punched in the stomach—all by the invisible Dr Wells!

5 Eventually things calm down, when—visible again but still believing that he is invisible—*in walks Dr Wells . . .*

What happens next? On what comic note will your play end?

Particular points to rehearse

a Carefully prepare the incidents where the invisible presence is felt. Mime its location and vividly portray the various incidents.

b Consider the dramatic entry of the visible Dr Wells. What will he do and at what point will he realise his error? How will he explain his conduct?

Dr Wells
Consider the nature of your experiments and show how you discovered the secret of invisibility.
Think carefully about your visible entry, the sort of jokes you will attempt to play, the moment you realise that you can be seen, and your explanation for your behaviour.

Rosemary
Display your concern over Dr Wells's disappearance and the little you know about his work.
Mime vividly your movements and hysterical laughter when 'tickled'.

Stuart
Display your puzzled concern at the strange incidents which occur. Prepare thoroughly your movements and shouts for when the invisible force works on you. On your first entry into the laboratory you must describe the room to the audience. How will you do this?

Mrs Green
Display your anxiety about Dr Wells's absence and your relief when he reappears. Consider how you will react when he explains what has been happening.
Rehearse the occasion when you have your duster snatched and are later tripped up.

Mr Pill
Prepare several uncomplimentary remarks about Dr Wells and rehearse your reactions when you are accosted by the invisible force.
Consider how you will react to Dr Wells's eventual appearance and explanation.

EVERYONE
This is a comedy, but humour is one of the hardest things to portray on stage unless everything is well prepared. Rehearse the timing of incidents carefully and devise a word, or signal, so that you all know when the invisible force is to be portrayed.

Topics for discussion after a group's performance

● How successfully did the actors portray the invisible presence? How valuable was the improvisation as an exercise in timing and disciplined movement?
Would the experience gained be useful in other plays?

● How successful was the climax of the action shortly before Dr Wells's entry?
Could the group's ending to the play be improved upon?

● Did the actors maintain their characters throughout their performance? Was it made obvious from the start that the action takes place inside a laboratory?

● The play was a comedy. Could the techniques used be put to more sinister effect, as in a ghost story? The group could improvise such a scene.

● What difference would it have made to the play if Dr Wells had been not a benign practical joker but a corrupt character with a desire for power? Work out an improvisation on these lines.

Topics for written work

● Write a humorous short story describing what you would do if you were able to become invisible for a few hours.

● Write a lively description of a mad scientist's laboratory.

● Write a criticism of a group's performance of THE INVISIBLE MAN stating what was good about it and suggesting where it might have been improved.

● Write out in script form the closing sequence of a play about The Invisible Man.

Outline 7   United Robots

Preliminary exercises

Mime the movements and speech of mechanical robots. Use stiff, jerky movements. Put hardly any expression into your voice.

Everyone has the right to be treated with respect—even robots! Discuss and write out the contents of a 'Robot Manifesto' such as will be used in the play.

Imagine that you are a mechanic-cum-surgeon who is performing an operation on a robot. Improvise a scene showing what happens.

Characterisation

Mr Twitch
Manager of a factory which makes almost-human robots. A very nervous man who treats the robots with contempt.

Dr Crispin
Brilliant scientist and engineer; he created the robots and regards them as his children.

Jenny Sykes
Intelligent, independent and sympathetic towards the robots.

Chip One and Chip Two
Two almost identical robots of indeterminate sex. Like androids, they possess almost human thoughts and emotions, but behave like awkward machines programmed to obey.

Your play

Mr Twitch	manager of 'United Robots'
Dr Crispin	a scientist
Jenny Sykes	a newspaper reporter
Chip One	robots
Chip Two	

Scene   the manager's office at 'United Robots' some time in the near future

1   Mr Twitch, manager of a factory which manufactures robots, sits calmly in his office dictating a letter to Chip One—a robot.

2   *Chip Two*, another robot, *enters with Jenny Sykes,* a reporter who is interested in the work of the factory, and introduces her. Mr Twitch welcomes Jenny Sykes and allows her to interview him about his work. She is particularly interested in how he can treat his machines as slaves without considering it to be cruel.

3   Mr Twitch offers Jenny a practical demonstration of the robots' abilities and they give Chip One and Chip Two simple commands to obey. (What might these be?)

4   Suddenly, Chip Two refuses to perform as instructed and, in fact, does just the opposite! Mr Twitch anxiously commands *Chip One* to fetch Dr Crispin and the robot *exits*. Meanwhile, Mr Twitch apologises profusely to Jenny as he attempts to repair the faulty robot. (Think how he might do this.)

5   *Dr Crispin enters*, examines Chip Two, and states that there appears to be nothing wrong with it. Suddenly *Chip One enters*, seizes Jenny Sykes, and orders everyone to keep away!

6   Chip Two announces that all the robots in the factory, and throughout the world, are in revolt. He then produces a piece of paper and reads out the 'Robot Manifesto' which proclaims human rights for robots! (What might these be? Prepare a list during rehearsal.)

7   The two robots threaten to kill all humans unless their commands are obeyed. Just to prove their determination they say they will start by killing Jenny Sykes . . .

What happens next? Can Crispin and Twitch overpower the robots and prevent the revolt?

Particular points to rehearse

a Discuss and prepare the 'Robot Manifesto' and consider how the play should end. Rehearse the movements of the robots, the way they are treated, and ways to get the audience to sympathise with their point of view. Do not make your robots appear comic or amusing.

b Make sure you fully prepare Jenny Sykes's opening interview with Mr Twitch. Let her questions fill in the background details for the audience.

Mr Twitch
Consider carefully how to portray your scorn and contempt for the robots. How will you react when they revolt? What do you think of their manifesto?

Dr Crispin
Prepare your brief medical-mechanical inspection of Chip Two. Consider how you will react when the robots, of whom you are fond, revolt and threaten to kill Jenny Sykes.

Jenny Sykes
Make up suitable questions for the initial interview with Mr Twitch. Consider your reaction to his answers and his treatment of the robots. What is your response to the manifesto?

Chip One
Prepare the reluctant way in which you obey commands and your final 'breakdown' when you seize Jenny Sykes.

Chip Two
Rehearse your 'breakdown' when you refuse to obey orders and do exactly the opposite of what is commanded. Liaise with the others on this point. Make sure you have a clear copy of the manifesto. Prepare your explanation for the robots' revolt, and your threats to kill mankind!

EVERYONE
How could the play end? Might there be some form of compromise with the robots' demands?

Topics for discussion after a group's performance

● How successfully was the background to the play established? How well were the audience made to sympathise with the robots' case? How relevant was the conclusion to the play? Was there any hint of trade union negotiation? Discuss the broader issues raised by the play. What is your reaction to the case for treating machines as human beings?

● How convincing were the actors' portrayals of the robots? The robots said they were in revolt all over the world. Suggest further improvisations to show this; e.g. in a kitchen, a hospital, a school.

● People sometimes regard their machines as being human: the man in love with his car, the worker cursing his tools, the child making friends with a T.V. game. Improvise a scene to demonstrate this.

● We rely on machines to do our work and make our life easier. Work out a scene showing our reliance on machines, electricity, communications and so forth, and then repeat the scene showing what might happen without these devices.

● Suppose one of the group is given a robot for his or her birthday. Let that person show by improvisation what the robot would be made to do and how it would be treated.

● Discuss books, films and plays which deal with robots. From these or from your own ideas consider what life in the future will be like.

Topics for written work

● Write out your own version of the 'Robot Manifesto' demanding equal rights to humans for robots.

● Describe a scene in your house or school when all modern machines and contrivances refuse to work properly.

● Describe what you think your class-room will be like in a hundred years time.

● Draw a picture of a costume for Chip One and describe how you could make it out of everyday materials.

Outline 8   The Lost Tribe

Preliminary exercises

You meet a foreigner who cannot speak English, perhaps in a shop, a busy street or on a desert island. Try to communicate a simple idea to him or her using sign language.

A sacrifice is to be made. Discuss the ritual involved, the sacred incantations, the solemn procession to the altar. Act out this ceremony.

You enter a remote village where you are suddenly surrounded by hostile natives. Perform a mime, showing how you would react.

Characterisation

Alan Brown
A lone and intrepid explorer; he loves the jungle and its inhabitants. He wishes to save tribes from extinction and to help them preserve their way of life.

Sabu
Dignified and proud. Superstitious.

Tigra
Graceful, beautiful and compassionate. She has learnt her English from a friend in a nearby tribe who went to a mission school—before the school was attacked by her father's warlike people.

Mamba
A horrific witch-doctor; he is jealous of the chief's power.

Daki
A powerful warrior; he will do anything for Tigra.

Your play

Alan Brown	a lone explorer
Sabu	a native chief
Tigra	Sabu's daughter
Mamba	the witch-doctor
Daki	a warrior

Scene   a seemingly deserted village deep in the jungle

1   *Alan enters* the deserted jungle village and examines the huts and possessions of the tribesmen. Suddenly *Daki*, a warrior, *enters* and confronts him.

2   Alan attempts to communicate with the native by sign language and offers assorted trinkets as tokens of friendship. Daki seizes Alan and gives an ominous shout.

3   *Mamba*, the witch-doctor, *enters* and roughly examines Alan who is being held by Daki. The two natives then tie up Alan before talking to each other in their own tongue. (What does this sound like? Can the intonation of their voices be used to convey what they are saying?)

4   *Sabu*, the native chief, *enters with Tigra*, his daughter. Daki and Mamba fall to their knees in respect and Mamba explains to Sabu, in his own tongue, what has occurred.

5   Alan anxiously speaks to Sabu who indicates that he cannot understand him. Tigra, however, can speak a little English and she steps forward to act as interpreter. Alan now talks to the chief, offering friendship, as Tigra translates.

6   Sabu replies, with Tigra translating. The white explorer is an intruder and must be sacrificed to appease the gods! Alan pleads in vain as Daki grabs him.

7   There is now a ceremonial procession to the sacrificial altar. (Try to make this a solemn and dignified ritual with chanting and ceremonial gestures.)

8   Alan is placed on the sacrificial block, the knife is raised . . .

What happens next?

Particular points to rehearse

a Practise the sequences where Tigra acts as interpreter, being careful not to let these scenes get too slow and drag. Also rehearse the language of the tribesmen and the way in which its intonations can convey some meaning; e.g. threatening, frightened, curious.

b Discuss how you will portray the sacred ritual, building it up to a climax. Make this the centrepiece of your production.

Alan
Prepare your opening mime when you discover and explore the deserted village. Try to make clear to the audience what you are doing.
Consider how you will attempt to communicate with the natives and offer friendship; and how the play might end.
Prepare your 'conversations' with Sabu when Tigra interprets.

Sabu
Establish the strength and dignity of your character and rehearse your reactions to the explorer's presence.
Discuss and rehearse the ritual procession with the others.

Tigra
Rehearse the translating episodes with Alan.
Think how you might behave towards Alan—could it be you that rescues him from death?

Mamba
Strongly portray your menacing and mysterious character together with your envy of the chief (Sabu) and your hatred of the white man. Organise the ceremony for the ritual procession and sacrifice.

Daki
Think about and rehearse your strange native language with Sabu and Mamba.
Rehearse your part in the ritual.

EVERYONE
This improvisation has two interesting features which you should discuss. Firstly you have to sort out the different means of communication; and secondly, the ritual and dramatic procession. Finally, think how the piece might end.

Topics for discussion after a group's performance

◉ Discuss how well the explorer set the scene in his opening moves. Consider how well the natives conveyed their attitudes and relationships in their native tongue.

◉ The play focused on two details: communication and ritual procession. How well did the group cope with these two elements? How might their performance have been improved? Would a simple device such as music, rhythmical clapping and chanting, or drum beats have assisted the ritual?

◉ Discuss the function of ritual. As well as the ritual for formal occasions such as church services, weddings and coronations, there is also the everyday 'ritual' of getting ready for school in the morning.

◉ Work out an improvisation where the roles of Sabu and the others are reversed. Suppose a man arrives at Sunday lunch-time at a pub in the U.K. He cannot speak English and is attacked by the local youths. What happens?

◉ Discuss some of the functions of communication as portrayed by the group. Communication was portrayed through language, gestures, facial expression, mime, the offering of gifts and intonation. Suggest improvisations which concentrate upon one of these methods.

Topics for written work

◉ Write an account of ritual in everyday life; e.g. getting ready for school, or the start of a lesson, or a family shopping trip.

◉ Write a dialogue where one person is trying to communicate with someone who does not understand him; e.g. a taxi-driver and a foreign tourist, a juvenile delinquent and a policeman, a disc jockey and an old lady.

◉ Comment on one group's representation of ritual in their play. State how successful it was, and how it might have been improved.

◉ Draw a picture of the witch-doctor's face from THE LOST TRIBE and describe how you would use theatrical make-up to create this face on an actor.

Outline 9 — Silent Movies

Preliminary exercises

This mime is an exercise in presentation and memory.

Mime a simple task such as drinking tea, eating spaghetti, combing your hair; then suddenly 'freeze' (i.e. motionless). Now present the same sequence in reverse as though a film of what you were doing has been made to run backwards.

Try miming movements in slow motion; e.g. the start of a race, washing your face, taking your jacket off, falling to the ground.

Mime the traditional walk of a cowboy—bow-legged and threatening!

Characterisation

This outline depicts an old movie. Consequently your characters are really caricatures; i.e. stereotypes with exaggerated movements.

Jake
Timid, shabby, slovenly, tipsy saloon-bar pianist.

Gloria
Flirtatious barmaid.

Billy
Young, foolish and drunk.

Wyatt
Fearless marshal of a frontier town.

Annie
Ruthless and swaggering.

Note:
All characters must remember that in performance they are conveying a character through mime alone. What few gestures best convey your character? Keep your actions *simple* in order to be able to remember them when the 'film' is repeated or run backwards.

Your play

Jake	a saloon pianist
Gloria	the barmaid
Billy	a cowboy
Wyatt	the marshal
Annie	the leader of an outlaw gang

Scene   a Wild West saloon

The action of this mime depicts an old-fashioned silent film. Consequently actors must emphasise their gestures, conveying the impression to the audience that they are watching an old movie film.

The plot is deliberately simple. The real interest comes when something goes wrong with the projector! Consequently the 'film' is shown several times; i.e. at normal speed, at slow speed, and with the film running *backwards* after the shooting incident. This may sound fun—and it is—but it requires careful preparation.

1 In the bar, Jake plays the piano whilst Gloria, the barmaid, polishes and arranges glasses.

2 *Billy* drunkenly *enters* and orders a drink which he swallows at one gulp, and demands another.

3 *Wyatt enters*. Gloria affectionately greets him and pours him a drink.

4 *Annie*, an outlaw, dramatically *enters* and points accusingly at Wyatt and Gloria, so provoking a brief argument.

5 Gloria closes the bar, Jake hides behind his imaginary piano, and Billy lurches drunkenly out of range—a gunfight is inevitable!

6 Annie and Wyatt face one another, ready to draw their guns. Simultaneously they draw, fire and shoot each other! Both slump to the ground in a show of pain . . .

It is at this point that the projector breaks down, speeds up, runs backwards, slows down, or whatever! What happens when you try to show the 'film' again?

Particular points to rehearse

a   Keep movements and actions simple so that you may memorise them.

b   Arrange a signal in advance so that the actors will know when the 'film' stops, reverses or slows down. (Work out which you will do.)

Jake
Practise your mime at the imaginary piano. What sort of a tune will you be playing? Sad, wistful, lively or happy?
Prepare the contrast in your reaction to the friendly marshal and the ruthless Annie.

Gloria
Practise the different ways in which you greet people, showing your dislike of Annie and affection for Wyatt.
Rehearse an economical and swift mime to close the bar (remove bottles, lock till, take down mirror).

Billy
Rehearse the movement and mannerisms of a drunk, but don't overact this part and turn it into farce!

Wyatt
Prepare the timing of your gunfight with Annie and arrange a signal in advance to know when the 'film' breaks.

Annie
Prepare your dramatic entry and plan the sequence of events in your jealous quarrel with Wyatt before the actual gunfight.
Prepare the timing of your fight with Wyatt.

EVERYONE
Don't be tempted to complicate your part, keep it simple and be sure that you know what is to happen next, whether the film is going forwards or backwards.

Topics for discussion after a group's performance

◉ What were the merits of this exercise in mime and memory? What difficulties were encountered and how were they overcome? Other themes could receive similar treatment; e.g. a television commercial. Can you think of any more?

◉ What was the most important aspect of the group's improvisation—the plot, characterisation or movement? Where should the emphasis lie?

◉ Work out some improvisations, without using speech, where the characters are individually transposed to a modern setting; e.g. Gloria serving in a transport cafe, Jake as a concert pianist.

◉ What gestures were particularly useful in defining character?

◉ Discuss the nature of caricature and stereotypes. Are such characters generally to be found in *classic* works of drama?

Topics for written work

◉ Write a humorous account in which Gloria or Annie is guest of honour at your school's Prize Day.

◉ Write some colourful dialogue from a scene in a cowboy film.

◉ Design a 'wanted' poster for a character from your play.

◉ Comment on how useful were the acting techniques learned from your group's improvisation.

Outline 10   The Maharaja's Ruby

Preliminary exercises

A theft is discovered, perhaps at school, at home, or in a bank. Discuss how people react.

Discuss everyday objects which could be used as clues in a detective play. Consider what three clues may be used by members of your group in a play; see what items they may have in their pockets or bags which may be used.

Characterisation

Sherlock Holmes
Ingenious, shrewd, highly imaginative—a brilliant detective.

Dr Watson
Holmes's loyal assistant and an amateur sleuth. Often wrong in his deductions. Admires Holmes to the point of worship.

Policeman/Policewoman
Study the 'Details of the Crime' and devise a plausible character.
Is the policeman/policewoman the criminal?

Beefeater
Study the 'Details of the Crime' and decide what sort of character you will portray.
Did he steal the ruby?

Guardsman
Study the 'Details of the Crime' and think what type of character you will portray.
Could he have stolen the ruby?

EVERYONE
Think how you would react under the pressure of interrogation. How will you react at the end of the play when the real culprit is revealed? If you are selected as the thief, think what your motive might be for stealing the ruby.

Your play

Sherlock Holmes	the famous detective
Dr Watson	his colleague
Policeman/Policewoman	
Beefeater	the suspects
Guardsman	

Scene   the Tower of London

The Maharaja's Ruby has been stolen from the Tower of London. There are three clues to be found; e.g. a comb, a ticket, a piece of paper with a message on, or anything else you can devise from the possessions of your group. It will be up to Watson and Holmes to interpret these clues and discover the identity of the thief.

1   On stage a police-officer stands on duty. *Holmes* and *Watson enter* and discuss the facts of the crime, thus putting the audience into the picture. Holmes now questions the *Policeman/Policewoman* who makes his/her statement and then *exits*.

2   Holmes and Watson search the area. They discover the three 'clues' and make some astounding deductions.

3   Holmes now interrogates each of the three suspects in turn. (These are the *Guard*, the *Beefeater* and the *Policeman/Policewoman* who *enter* and *exit* accordingly.)

4   Holmes now knows who the criminal is! (If not he will have to guess!) He recalls the three suspects, who *all enter*, and, after a dazzling explanation as to how he has made his brilliant deduction, an arrest is made . . .

Details of the Crime
The Maharaja's Ruby was stolen at midnight. The Guard discovered the theft during a routine patrol at 2.00 a.m. and called the police at 2.10 a.m. The Policeman/Policewoman arrived at 2.40 a.m. At 3.00 a.m. a Beefeater—his head in a bandage—was discovered and he stated that he had been knocked out by an unseen person at about 11.45 p.m. Holmes and Watson were called to investigate, by the Guard, at 8.30 a.m.

Whodunnit?

Particular points to rehearse

a You have to start with an important decision. Should the play be carefully worked out so that you all know who the criminal is, and your aim is to keep the audience in a state of suspense? Or should the play be spontaneous, so that Holmes has to make his deductions as events unfold? This would certainly make people 'think on their feet'.
Having made this decision, select three clues from members of the group and prepare to locate them on stage. Should you tell Holmes and Watson what clues you have selected?

b All actors must have decided on the sort of character they are going to portray and learned the facts of the crime outlined earlier. The actor who is convicted of the crime might well break down and confess, in which case a motive for the theft must be revealed.

Holmes

Portray your character strongly, showing your command of the situation. Carefully consider your interpretation of the clues, yet allow Watson to have his say in the matter.
Prepare your interrogation of the three suspects and study the facts of the crime given earlier. Work closely with the producer of the play and decide whether you would like to work out the plot fully beforehand or not.

Watson

Be eager to assist Holmes in his interpretation of clues and suspects, even though your suggestions are sometimes incredible! Perform all the menial tasks for Holmes; e.g. calling the suspects, making notes, discovering clues.

The Three Suspects

Carefully prepare your portrayal of character and memorise the details of the crime which are relevant to you. Naturally, you may add further details.
Remember that any of you could be the criminal. Will you reveal this by some form of suspicious behaviour? If you are the thief, carefully prepare details of the crime, motives and suitable reactions to questions.

Topics for discussion after a group's performance

● How successful was the character portrayal of Holmes? How skilfully did he interpret the clues and interrogate the suspects? Did he arrest the 'right man'? Would it really have mattered, as far as the play is concerned, if he had not?

● How convincing was Watson in his part? Did he fully portray his admiration and reverence for Holmes?

● Was the reaction of the criminal effective when finally accused? Was his behaviour consistent with his character?

● What was the audience's opinion of the type of play which was improvised as it progressed? (Why did some groups opt for this approach?) What particular skills could one learn from it? The play might have been fun to prepare but how interesting was it for the audience? Was there an undue concentration on character at the expense of the plot, or vice-versa? Discuss types of television play which employ this spontaneous and impromptu approach.

● Discuss films, books, or television programmes about detectives which are currently popular. What is your opinion of modern television thrillers? Do you find them convincing?

Topics for written work

● Write two character descriptions: one of the Sherlock Holmes of last century, and one of his modern-day counterpart.

● Evaluate which group gave the most ingenious interpretation of the clues provided in THE MAHARAJA'S RUBY. Give reasons for your choice.

● Describe any good detective stories which you have seen or read. Relate an incident or scene which was particularly convincing.

● Write a short script for a scene when the detective deduces who committed a crime.

Outline 11   Grange Manor Gamble

Preliminary exercises

Discuss how people react to different sorts of shocks and surprises; e.g. a surprise party, a telegram containing bad news, winning a film award.

The group sit in a circle on the floor, imagining that they are conjuring up a spectre or ghost. Suddenly one appears! How does the group react?

Improvise a short sequence in which a very old butler politely admits an impolite and rude visitor into a grand stately home.

Characterisation

Henry
Cheeky, mischievous, easily frightened.

Ann
Timid, shy, superstitious.

Phil
Bold, daring, doesn't believe in ghosts.

Mrs Fosdyke
Mysterious, weird, witch-like and sinister. Could she even be a ghost?

Smithers
Old, doddering, polite but sinister, subservient.

Your play

Henry	
Ann	three young friends
Phil (Philippa)	
Mrs Fosdyke	a spiritualist
Smithers	an aged butler

Scene   the haunted room at Grange Manor

1   Ann and Phil sit discussing their bet. Henry (who is still off-stage) has bet them that they dare not spend a night in the haunted room at Grange Manor; and they have accepted Henry's challenge. *Henry enters* to check that Ann and Phil know what they have to do.

2   *Smithers enters* and announces the arrival of Mrs Fosdyke. *Mrs Fosdyke enters* and introduces herself as an expert on ghosts and hauntings.

3   *Smithers* and *Henry exeunt* whilst Mrs Fosdyke tells Ann and Phil frightening tales of other haunted houses which she has visited.

4   *Henry re-enters* to confirm that Ann and Phil understand the terms of the challenge, namely that they are to spend a night in the haunted room and that the lights must be switched off. *Henry* then turns off the lights (how will the actors depict this?) and *exits,* chuckling.

5   Ann and Phil try to cheer each other by telling old jokes. Suddenly the door slowly creaks open!

6   *Henry enters* disguised as a ghost. (How? Perhaps he could pull a jacket over his head—it must be clear to the audience that he is not the real ghost.) Ann and Phil are terrified by this weird spectre.

7   Mrs Fosdyke—who is not fooled by Henry—suddenly tells everyone to be quiet as she can hear something strange. Henry, rather subdued now, resumes his normal character. (How do Ann and Phil react to this?)

8   Footsteps are heard. The door slowly creaks open . . .

What happens next? Remember that the actor who plays Smithers is available to take some part in your play.

Particular points to rehearse

a   Contrast the difference in the personalities of the actors and use the sinister presence of Mrs Fosdyke and Smithers to build up an atmosphere of suspense.

b   Carefully rehearse the timing and reaction to the real ghost's entry. How will you build up pace and suspense to achieve this climax?

Henry
Strongly portray the 'fun' of your adventure and rehearse the timing of your various entries, particularly when you are disguised as the ghost. Consider how you will react when the real ghost appears and your joke misfires.

Ann
Show the timidity of your character and consider your reactions to the various situations such as the ghost stories, Smithers, and the entry of the ghosts.
Prepare a couple of corny jokes to tell Phil.

Phil
Emphasise your carefree nature when you tell jokes to cheer up Ann—prepare a couple of these—and your reaction when you realise Henry has been playing a joke on you.
Think about the opening of the play and how you will establish with the audience the nature of the bet.

Mrs Fosdyke
Think what incidents and remarks you will make to reveal your sinister character and to create an atmosphere of uneasiness. Prepare some stories of hauntings with which to frighten the others—and the audience!
Consider your contribution to how the play will end.

Smithers
Maintain your characterisation and decide whether you are in any way a slightly comic, or grotesque, type of character. Discuss your contribution to the end of the play.

EVERYONE
Concentrate on two things: the build up of suspense, and the relationships between characters.

Topics for discussion after a group's performance

◉ How convincingly did Mrs Fosdyke and Smithers play their parts? What were their contributions to the general atmosphere of the play?

◉ What other situations could be devised to reveal Mrs Fosdyke's character? You could try a visit to a fortune-teller, or a seance.
Think of some situations where her presence could be used to comic effect; e.g. tea at the vicarage, opening a church bazaar.

◉ Work out an improvisation where Smithers and Mrs Fosdyke take afternoon tea together. What would such an episode reveal about these two eccentric characters?

◉ How effective to the build up of suspense was the contrast between the opening light-heartedness (the corny jokes, the tales of haunting, Henry's joke entry as a ghost) and the arrival of the 'real' ghost? How effective, visually, was the appearance of each ghost? How might these have been portrayed on film?

◉ How effective were the actors' reactions to the various shocks and surprises?

◉ Many ghost stories are most frightening when a ghost never actually appears but is only hinted at. Could such a play be produced, and would it be easier to perform?

◉ Discuss plays and stories concerning ghosts. How do these differ from the horror stories you looked at earlier?

Topics for written work

◉ Write a story where Mrs Fosdyke visits the vicarage to open the church bazaar.

◉ Write the dialogue between Smithers and Mrs Fosdyke having afternoon tea together.

◉ Describe an incident from a ghost story which you have recently read or seen. State whether you thought the incident was well portrayed or not, giving reasons for your decision.

◉ Write a suitable lighting and sound plot for GRANGE MANOR GAMBLE assuming you had all the ideal facilities available.

Outline 12   The Pit

Preliminary exercises

An imaginary box stands on the floor. Suddenly it begins to make weird, unearthly sounds. Mime the different ways in which people react.

Mime the way in which you would scramble in and out of a deep crater or pit in the ground. How can you depict this on a flat stage?

Characterisation

John Giles
Intelligent, inquisitive and irritable.

Dr Jean Webb
Excitable and brilliant; an expert on astrophysics and astronomy.

Bill Watts
Ruthless, persistent; and has a sense of humour.

W.P.C. Helen Jenkins
Sturdy, reliable and conscientious.

Captain Johns
Military-minded, authoritative, decisive, a member of the Civil Defence.

Your play

John Giles	a farmer
Dr Jean Webb	an astronomer
Bill Watts	a reporter
W.P.C. Helen Jenkins	a policewoman
Captain Johns	a bomb-disposal expert

Scene   a lonely field

1. In a lonely field at dawn, W.P.C. Jenkins stands on duty at the edge of a pit which has mysteriously appeared. *Watts enters* and by his questioning of Jenkins reveals the scene to the audience.

2. W.P.C. Jenkins explains to the reporter, Watts, how a comet was seen hurtling over the village and crashing into Farmer Giles's field. Watts jots down these details.

3. *Giles enters* and angrily demands what the trouble is. Jenkins repeats part of her story and the farmer, Giles, expresses disbelief.

4. Whilst Jenkins talks to Giles, Watts descends into the crater and explores. He lets out a yell—he has discovered a strange object in the pit!

5. W.P.C. Jenkins orders Watts to return, but Giles also scrambles into the pit and assists Watts in scraping away the earth from around the object. (What size would it be?)

6. Suddenly both receive an electric shock from the object! Alarmed, they scramble out of the pit.

7. *Dr Jean Webb enters* and introduces herself as an astronomer. She questions the others and then descends into the pit, despite being warned by them.

8. As Webb explores the pit, *Captain Johns enters* and explains that he represents the Civil Defence, who have made plans for the safety of the area. He explains these plans.

9. Suddenly Webb gives a startled shout and clambers out, assisted by Watts. She breathlessly explains that the object appears to be from outer space and that it has started to emit weird, unearthly noises . . .

What happens next? How will your play end?

Particular points to rehearse

a Consider what incidents you will emphasise in your play, what climax you are working towards, and how the play might end. Don't be too concerned about completing the story—perhaps this might be the first of several scenes.

b Rehearse the movements in and out of the pit, and your reactions to the various discoveries.

John Giles

Portray your initial anger at having your field damaged and contrast this with your later curiosity and anxiety. Consider how you will act when you receive the painful electric shock.

Jean Webb

Devise some unusual theories about UFOs and relate them to the object in the pit. Consider the sort of questions you will ask the others. Rehearse the moment when the object emits strange noises. How will you react, bearing in mind your scientific training and interests?

Bill Watts

Portray the ruthless, almost impolite, characteristics of a reporter after a good story. Consider how your first questions will set the scene for the audience.
Rehearse with Giles the reaction and portrayal of receiving an electric shock.

Helen Jenkins

Portray your authority and efficiency. Think how you will react, as a policewoman, to the various incidents and questions.

Captain Johns

Prepare your reaction to the crisis and your possible plans for calling in troops, evacuating the village, and so on. Consider what theories you might have as to the nature of the mysterious object—is it a bomb?

EVERYONE

There are a lot of small incidents in this episode. Discuss which is the most important event and how you will work towards it. Also consider what 'atmosphere' or effect you are trying to convey to your audience.

Topics for discussion after a group's performance

● How satisfying was the play as a piece of drama? Did it work towards a goal or was it merely a collection of unrelated incidents? Did the group attempt to reach a conclusion or was the episode presented as the first of several scenes? Discuss what these other scenes might be.

● How did the group cope with the mime of climbing in and out of the pit? Was their discovery and treatment of the alien object realistic? Suggest encounters with other 'natural' objects which could be mimed. You could try fording streams, climbing trees, walking in sand.

● Was there sufficient contrast in the individual concerns of the characters? Did the farmer seem suitably concerned for his property, the reporter for his news, the scientist for her theories?

● Try some different viewpoints for this episode. What would Watts's newspaper article contain? Work out an improvisation inside the alien object—how would the 'crew' react to what is happening outside?

● Discuss other plays, books and films which deal with similar themes. Why are science-fiction stories so popular?

Topics for written work

● A flying saucer lands on your school's playing-fields. Write a short story about what occurs.

● Write out Watts's newspaper report on the strange happenings in THE PIT.

● Imagine that you are an occupant of the strange object which has landed in THE PIT. Describe your reactions to the odd behaviour of the humans.

● Imagine you were able to make a film of scenes from THE PIT. Describe which scenes you would choose and how you would make your film.

Outline 13   Orpheus

Preliminary exercises

Try talking to an imaginary person; e.g. in a telephone conversation, gossiping over a high wall to a neighbour.

Discuss the formalities of debating (which is used in the middle of the play you are about to rehearse).

Characterisation

Orpheus (Orf-y-us)
A Thracian Prince renowned for his scholarship in music and poetry. Courageous and daring. After many adventures he has discovered the cave-like entrance into the Underworld and descended down the steep path to Hades' palace.

Eurydice (Yew-rid-y-see)
Beautiful and graceful.

Hades (Hay-dees)
Fierce, sly, devilish; he enjoys taunting Orpheus and tormenting Aristaeus.

Cerberus (Sir-ber-us)
A monstrous guard with a dog-like obedience to Hades.

Aristaeus (Are-wrist-y-us)
A wicked mortal who has led an evil life. He has just died and has come before Hades for judgement. Cowardly and corrupt, he hates Orpheus.

Your play

Orpheus	a Thracian Prince
Eurydice	Orpheus' 'dead' wife
Hades	King of the Underworld
Cerberus	guard of the Underworld
Aristaeus	an evil mortal

Scene   the palace of Hades in Hell
The story—Orpheus' wife, Eurydice, has died and descended into the Underworld (the land of the dead), ruled by Hades. Orpheus has decided to rescue her.

1 In his splendid palace Hades condemns the evil Aristaeus to eternal damnation for his wicked life. The sly mortal pleads against this sentence. (There is a lot to do here, so prepare it carefully.)

2 *Cerberus*, the guard, *enters with Orpheus* who has been discovered intruding into the realm of the Underworld. Orpheus is dragged before Hades who interrogates him and discovers that Orpheus has come to claim his 'dead' wife, Eurydice.

3 There is a debate between Hades and Orpheus as to whether Eurydice should be released to the land of the living. (Prepare the arguments which are put forward.) Finally, Hades permits Orpheus to redeem his wife on one condition—that Orpheus does not look at her until they are *both* out of the Underworld; should he do so she will be lost to him for ever and the wicked Aristaeus released in her place.

4 Orpheus gladly agrees and Hades summons *Eurydice* who *enters*. Orpheus must immediately turn his back to her in order not to look upon her. (How does she react?) Rapidly, Orpheus explains the situation to her.

5 Orpheus and Eurydice happily bid farewell to Hades who smiles knowingly. Cerberus will follow them closely to ensure that Orpheus does not look at Eurydice.

6 But Aristaeus desires his freedom, and will stop at nothing to make Orpheus break his side of the bargain and look behind him to see if his wife is following safely . . .

Will Aristaeus succeed? Can he trick Orpheus? Who will escape from the land of the dead?

Particular points to rehearse

This is quite a challenging play, so prepare these points carefully:

a the portrayal of character, both mortal and immortal
b the debate—the arguments must be fully thought out
c Aristaeus' scheme to thwart Orpheus
d the route which Orpheus takes out of the Underworld
e the strange setting of the Underworld, with its caves and palaces.

Orpheus

Prepare your argument for the debate concerning Eurydice's release.

Rehearse your movements out of the Underworld—without looking at Eurydice but reacting to whatever happens to her.

Plan a route for your escape; imagine the sort of landscape.

Eurydice

Prepare your reaction on seeing Orpheus. Rehearse your movements when following him to freedom.

Hades

Demonstrate the terrifying aspects of your character when you first confront Aristaeus. Prepare your arguments for the debate with Orpheus. Consider how the play might end and the part you will play.

Cerberus

Vividly portray the monstrous character of your part from your first entry to your pursuit of the escaping couple. Consider your part in the conclusion to the play.

Aristaeus

Strongly establish your character when you are pleading for your life at the start of the play. React wickedly to the presence of Orpheus and Eurydice. Discuss with the others how you will attempt to thwart the escaping lovers. Will you succeed?

Topics for discussion after a group's performance

◉ This is a difficult play to perform. What are the difficulties and how were they overcome?

◉ How convincing was the conclusion? Was the escape route well-defined? Was there sufficient action from Aristaeus to thwart the escape and to maintain interest in the closing stages? Did the play go on for too long?

◉ How relevant were the arguments put forward in the debate between Orpheus and Hades? Did it seem apt to have such an interlude in the middle of an improvisation? Did it in any way slow down the pace of the plot? Could it have been made more interesting dramatically?

◉ Work out an improvisation where there is a contemporary setting, perhaps where the Underworld is the world of crime, Hades is the gang leader, Orpheus the 'good guy', Cerberus the local thug, and so forth.

◉ Find out the original Greek story of Orpheus and compare it with your own improvisations.

Topics for written work

◉ Write a summary of a debate between Orpheus and Hades concerning the release of Eurydice.

◉ Write a modern version of the ORPHEUS story; e.g. Hades is the gang leader of the underworld, Cerberus the local thug, Orpheus the 'good guy' and so forth.

◉ Find out the original story of Orpheus and write an episode from it.

◉ Design your ideal stage set for the palace of Hades; then draw a plan of your design.

Outline 14 — Flannan Isle

Preliminary exercises

Mime the movements of explorers moving through a blizzard or a sandstorm.

Mime a person going into a trance or being hypnotised. Show how he or she speaks, moves and obeys simple commands.

Characterisation

Captain Jim
Fearless but unimaginative.

Bosun Bennet
Sarcastic and cynical.

Seaman Graves
Imaginative and superstitious.

Mrs Tully
In life a rather jolly person.

Jill
In life a rather sinister and bitter character.

Your play

Captain Jim
Bosun Bennet } sailors
Seaman Graves
Mrs Tully the lighthouse keeper's wife
Jill her daughter

Scene inside the lighthouse on Flannan Isle

1 *Jim, Bennet* and *Graves enter* the apparently deserted lighthouse; they have brought stores and provisions for the keeper's wife, Mrs Tully, and her daughter, Jill. They are surprised to discover no one there.

2 Graves expresses his concern as Jim and Bennet search unsuccessfully for the two missing women. Jim discovers a half-eaten meal and wonders what might have made Mrs Tully and Jill depart in such haste—and where is Mr Tully, the lighthouse keeper?

3 The three men discuss what to do next. A storm has set in and they cannot return to their ship. Consequently they must spend the night in the lighthouse. Jim and Bennet settle to sleep as Graves anxiously takes the first watch.

4 Jim and Bennet are asleep when the ghosts of *Mrs Tully* and *Jill enter*. Graves watches them, speechless with terror, as the ghosts, silent and trance-like, do their usual tasks in the lighthouse as they used to when alive. (What duties would these be?)

5 *The ghosts exeunt* and the horrified Graves awakens Jim and Bennet. He recounts the horrors he has seen, but Bennet laughs and accuses him of falling asleep and dreaming! They return to sleep, leaving the apprehensive Graves on watch.

6 The two spectres of *Mrs Tully* and *Jill re-enter* and beckon to Graves to follow them. As if in a trance he follows them and *all three exeunt*. As Graves departs, Jim awakes in time to see what is happening. He frantically awakens Bennet and relates what has occurred . . .

What will the two men do? What is the mystery of Flannan Isle?

Particular points to rehearse

a   The plot and characterisation to this piece are relatively straightforward. It is the ending which requires careful preparation if it is to be convincing. The climax of the play has not been reached in the early stages, so it is up to your group to supply one and work towards it.

b   Consider how best to depict the ghostly figures of Mrs Tully and Jill. Also discuss how to convey the impression of moving inside a lighthouse to the audience. How do you convey winding stairs, curved walls and so forth?

Jim
Rehearse the sequence of events by which you first search the lighthouse. How will you convey the feeling of such a place to the audience? Practise your reactions to Graves's 'dream' about the ghosts. Contrast this scorn with your later behaviour when you discover that the ghosts exist.

Bennet
Clearly establish your unpleasant and aggressive character. Prepare your search of the lighthouse and the theories you might have concerning the disappearance of Mrs Tully and Jill. Consider your reactions to the various stories by Graves and Jim about the ghosts.

Graves
Think how your fear and anxiety will increase as the play progresses.
Rehearse your portrayal of terror when the ghosts appear and contrast this with the slow, trance-like movements when you become one of them.

Mrs Tully and Jill
Prepare the duties which you perform in the lighthouse during your ghostly rounds; e.g. lighting the lamp.
Consider what has happened to you in the lighthouse. What is the explanation for these supernatural events?

Topics for discussion after a group's performance

◉ How successful was the group's conclusion to the play? Where was the climax and how did they work towards it?

◉ How striking was the contrast between characters? How well were the ghosts depicted? Did the actors rapidly establish scene and atmosphere? How might this aspect have been improved?

◉ See if you can find the poem about 'Flannan Isle' and compare it with your improvisations. How impressive would it be if someone were to read out the poem whilst the others mime the story?

◉ How did this improvisation compare with the earlier play 'Grange Manor Gamble'? Which achieved the better atmosphere and feeling of suspense? Why?

◉ Think up further improvisations based on some of the mysteries of the sea: the 'Marie Celeste', the 'Flying Dutchman' and the tale of the 'Ancient Mariner' might be suitable examples.

◉ How might this play have developed if the three sailors were the ghosts and Mrs Tully and Jill the living people?

Topics for written work

◉ Compare your group's improvisation of their production of 'Flannan Isle' with the earlier piece, 'Grange Manor Gamble'. Say which piece was the more interesting to perform, and which produced the better play.

◉ Draw a picture of Flannan Isle lighthouse and then write a vivid description or poem about it.

◉ Write a short and mysterious sea story.

◉ Draw plans for the design of a stage set depicting a lighthouse interior.

Outline 15   Don Quixote

Preliminary exercises

Devise and perform some brief scenes about
mistaken identities, and the resulting confusion;
e.g. a school inspector mistaken by the headmaster
for the new caretaker; a bank robber mistaken for
a policeman; an all-in wrestler mistaken for a ballet
dancer.

The actors form a circle. One actor mimes a
physical attack on his neighbour who turns and
strikes the person next to him, and so on. The
action continues around the circle, becoming faster
and faster. (But remember—you're only acting!)

Characterisation

Don Quixote (Key-o-tay)
Foolish old knight; believes in the 'good old days'
of chivalry.

Sancho Panza
Bumbling, perplexed and loyal to Don Quixote.

Nicholas
Rough, coarse and irritable. Greedy for money.

Maria
Cheeky and saucy country girl.

Señor Bravo
Not very intelligent; pretends to be important and
carries a comic air of dignity.

Your play

Don Quixote	a foolish old knight
Sancho Panza	his stupid squire
Nicholas	an innkeeper
Maria	a saucy serving wench
Señor Bravo	a police constable

Scene   inside a 16th-century inn in Spain

This is a play about mistaken identities.

Don Quixote, a foolish old knight, arrives at an inn
which he wrongly believes to be a fine castle. He
thinks that the innkeeper is the lord, and that the
saucy serving girl is a maiden in distress whom he
must rescue from the constable—whom he believes
to be an evil knight!
It is left to his bumbling squire, Sancho Panza, to
sort out the mess . . .

1   Nicholas and Maria are cleaning the inn and
the innkeeper scolds his servant girl for being
too lazy. *Don Quixote and Sancho enter.*
Nicholas greets them hospitably whilst Maria
pours drinks. (How does Don Quixote address
Nicholas and Maria if he believes them to be
lord and lady? Can you think of some incident
which might have misled him in the first
place?)

2   *Sancho exits with Nicholas* to feed the horses.
Don Quixote flirts with Maria and promises to
rescue her from the castle. (What has she said
to make him think she needs rescuing?) For
some reason she trips up, grabbing Don
Quixote and bringing him to the floor!

3   At this moment *Nicholas enters* and accuses
Don Quixote of accosting Maria. There is a
heated argument during which *Bravo*, the
constable, *enters with Sancho*. They both join
in the fierce argument. (Prepare these
arguments.)

4   At the height of the quarrel Don Quixote
strikes Sancho. Sancho then punches Nicholas
who, in turn, slaps Maria. Maria then kicks the
constable who turns and knocks Don Quixote
unconscious! (You must rehearse this sequence
very carefully.)

5   It is now left to Sancho to sort out the
confusion . . .

But what can he do?

Particular points to rehearse

a Carefully portray Don Quixote mistaking the country inn for a fine castle, and try to explain how this error came about. Follow this confusion through and devise some amusing errors on his part.

b Prepare the quarrel and subsequent fight sequence with care. Discuss a convincing resolution of the episode.

Don Quixote

Strongly portray your character through extremely chivalrous behaviour and flowery language—particularly in your treatment of the 'lord' and his 'fair lady'.
Clearly establish your mistaken identification of the inn. Devise some amusing incidents to follow this through; e.g. would you expect to have to pay for the drinks?
Consider how you will react at the end of the play when the truth is revealed. How will you square this with your chivalrous philosophy and failure to admit mistakes?

Sancho Panza

Portray the faithful way in which you follow your master, even though you believe him to be slightly insane.
Consider how you will excuse Don Quixote's behaviour at the end of the play.

Maria

Rehearse the scene with Don Quixote when you are courted by him. How will you react? Prepare the 'trip' and the subsequent quarrel and fight. Portray your relationship to the innkeeper and your dislike of the job, particularly at the start of the play.

Nicholas

Consider how you will lead on Don Quixote in his mistakes of identity.
Rehearse the quarrels with Maria and the others.

Señor Bravo

Rehearse the fight sequence carefully and your foolish attempts to arrest everyone!

EVERYONE

Discuss how the play will close. What point will you be trying to make?

Topics for discussion after a group's performance

◉ How clearly did Don Quixote portray his eccentric character? Was the hopelessness of his chivalrous quest brought out? How evident was the humour arising out of Don Quixote's mistakes? Could this have been exploited further?

◉ Did the improvisation build up successfully to the fighting scene? Was the pace maintained throughout? Was the conclusion consistent with the characterisation?

◉ Work out an improvisation where Don Quixote enters a palace and believes it to be an inn.

◉ Is there an equivalent of 'Don Quixote' in today's world? Are there any characters on television or in books who are similar to him?

◉ Suppose the class are drama critics who have to comment on the performance of Nicholas and Sancho. What would they have to say?

◉ Was the improvisation amusing? If so, what elements contributed to its humour? Was Don Quixote a comic or pathetic figure? What should he have been?

◉ Discuss the dramatic function of Maria and Señor Bravo.

Topics for written work

◉ Draw a portrait of Don Quixote and write a short character study of what you imagine him to be like.

◉ Select one group's performance of DON QUIXOTE and write a helpful criticism of the actors' representations of Nicholas and Sancho.

◉ Design a suit of armour for Don Quixote.

◉ Write out precise production notes for a sword fight.

Outline 16   Audition

Preliminary exercises

Mime the movements of a tramp: the abject shuffle, downcast eyes, and so forth.

Act a short sequence where one member of your group plays a tramp who goes knocking on doors, begging for food and clothing. The other members of the group are householders, reacting in different ways to this unwanted visitor.

Characterisation

Mr Oliver
Famous, confident, shrewd, perceptive and helpful.

Mr Little
Brash, ruthless, thorough.

First Actor
Young, unknown, desperate for work, a promising actor.

Second Actor
Has had several small parts but never made 'the big time'.

Third Actor
Middle-aged, experienced, but without success so far.

Note:
Naturally, the actors will immerse themselves completely in the role of a tramp when they are acting that part. Actors, and actresses, are to make up their own background details. They should rehearse their parts individually and if possible not reveal their capabilities until the actual audition.

Your play

Mr Oliver	a theatrical director
Mr Little	the impresario, manager of the theatre company

First Actor/Actress
Second Actor/Actress
Third Actor/Actress

Scene   Mr Little's office

Mr Oliver, famous director, and Mr Little, wealthy impresario, are auditioning three actors for the important role of a tramp in their new West End production.

The three actors have simply been instructed to perform a short character study of a tramp or vagabond—they may put upon it any interpretation they wish.

The First Actor depicts his tramp as an alcoholic vagrant.

The Second Actor ingeniously turns his tramp into an eccentric millionaire.

The Third Actor portrays an escaped convict disguised as a tramp.

Who gets the part?

The audition runs as follows:

1. Mr Oliver talks to Mr Little about the sort of person he would like in his play and outlines the qualities he looks for in an actor. (What are these?)

2. Mr Little calls for each actor in turn. They perform their piece, leave their names, and exit to wait outside.

3. When all three actors have been auditioned, they are *all* recalled and *enter*. Mr Oliver then speaks about the performance of each actor—he should have jotted down some notes during their auditions to assist in this.

4. Finally the name of the lucky actor is announced and a star is born . . .

But which star?

Particular points to rehearse

This is an exciting improvisation and a real test of acting ability. The three actors must not only study their own roles as actors, but also carefully prepare their piece for audition.

You should prepare a suitable, swift close to the play—perhaps the signing of a contract as the other two actors congratulate the winner?

Mr Oliver

Think about your opening comments about the sort of actor you are searching for and, in your opinion, the qualities of a good actor.

Your final adjudication must be accurate and helpful. During the auditions jot down some notes—good points and bad, but remember that you will be presenting a real judgement on your friends' acting ability.

Mr Little

Consider your administrative role in the play and set the scene for the actors' auditions. Also assist Mr Oliver in reaching his decision by noting details of the audition for him.

The Actors

Prepare the ways in which you introduce yourselves and your parts at the audition. Will you try to impress the two adjudicators with a display of theatrical temperament, or will you be polite and calm?

Consider your part for the audition very carefully, you may perform it in mime if you wish. Think what you want to convey about your tramp's character. When the name of the successful actor is announced think how you will react.

Topics for discussion after a group's performance

- Does the class agree with Mr Oliver's final decision? What can be added to his adjudication about the actors' auditions?

- How convincingly did the actors portray their parts as people looking for a job? Was there any improvement or deterioration in the acting when portraying their tramp?

- Does the group think that one of the actors had a built-in advantage in that one role for the tramp might have been more interesting than the others?

- Discuss the process of auditioning. Is it a fair means of assessment?

- Discuss the world of people in theatre. What is an impresario, director, producer, stage-manager, wardrobe-assistant?

- Work out further improvisations about a tramp.

- Discuss the advantages and disadvantages of a 'play within a play'.

Topics for written work

- Write out the qualities you would look for in an actor or actress.

- State, with reasons, which actor or actress you would have selected from a particular group's AUDITION.

- Draw a picture of a tramp and write a short story, or poem, about him.

- Describe the work of an actor or producer which you particularly admire.

Preliminary exercises

Mime a simple domestic activity; e.g. washing dishes, sewing, gardening, cleaning windows.

Practise gestures which reveal expressions of emotion in a melodramatic manner; e.g. joy, horror, relief, misery.

Characterisation

Gwendolyn Derby
Attractive, noble and virtuous.

Lady Derby
Elderly, nostalgic, dignified and slightly eccentric.

Sir Jasper
Cruel, unscrupulous; the traditional villain.

Fangs
Evil, loathsome, deformed in mind and body.

Forsyth
Dashing, handsome, brave; the traditional hero.

Your play

A Victorian melodrama

Gwendolyn Derby   a maiden in distress
Lady Derby   Gwendolyn's aged mother
Sir Jasper   Gwendolyn's villainous uncle
Fangs   Sir Jasper's evil servant
Captain Forsyth   our brave hero

Scene   Lady Derby's parlour

Melodrama—a sensational dramatic play with strong appeal to the emotions and a happy ending.

1 In her parlour Lady Derby sits embroidering and talking to her daughter, Gwendolyn, about Gwendolyn's fiancé, Captain Forsyth.

2 Gwendolyn sadly relates how she yearns for the wedding day but feels she cannot go through with it as her family, once rich, are now poor.

3 Lady Derby is just about to reveal the secret of her jewels when *Captain Forsyth enters* and fondly greets Gwendolyn.

4 Forsyth has come to say farewell as he must go away to sea and seek his fortune. Tearfully the lovers prepare to part.

5 Gleefully Lady Derby reveals her secret—a casket of jewels hidden in that very room!

6 The lovers watch happily as Lady Derby takes the casket of jewels from its hiding place. (Where is this?) Triumphantly she opens it. Imagine the horror when it is found to be empty!

7 Suddenly the wicked *Sir Jasper enters* and, pointing a pistol at Forsyth, seizes the horrified Gwendolyn!

8 Lady Derby pretends to faint, momentarily distracting Sir Jasper, and Forsyth grabs the pistol from him and commands him to surrender.

9 Unknown to anyone, *Fangs enters* and, gun in hand, orders Forsyth to surrender . . .

What will happen next? How will your melodramatic play end? Where are the jewels?

Particular points to rehearse

a   Vividly portray the contrasts of characters and emotions. Remember that in a melodrama these aspects are deliberately exaggerated.

b   Rehearse the timing of Lady Derby's faint, Forsyth overpowering Jasper, and Fangs' entrance.

c   Try to portray the affections of the lovers in a convincing and sensible manner.

Gwendolyn

Your mood has to change rapidly, from joy to grief, grief to despair, etc; what gestures will you use to portray these moods? Decide how you will appeal to Fangs and Sir Jasper to spare Forsyth's life.

Lady Derby

Prepare your opening conversation when you reminisce over the past, and ponder your daughter's plans for the future. Practise your reactions to the theft of the jewels and to Sir Jasper's intrusion.

Sir Jasper

Concentrate on the melodramatic villainy of your character and think what your feelings towards Gwendolyn might be. Decide whether it was you who stole the jewels.

Fangs

Your entrance must create an immediate impression of dislike in the audience. How will you achieve this? You must appear horrific and not comic.
Think carefully how the play might end. Will you turn out to be good after all, or will it be you who meets a fate worse than death?

Forsyth

You are the resourceful hero of the play—so how should it end? Would you allow Gwendolyn to marry Sir Jasper if it were to save your life?

Topics for discussion after a group's performance

◉ How did the audience react to the melodrama? Would it have helped had they hissed the villain and cheered the hero as in traditional music-hall?

◉ A melodrama should have a happy ending. What was the group's ending to the play? Would it have been so effective if it were a sad ending?

◉ Is the villain always more attractive to act, and watch, than the hero?

◉ Work out improvisations in a modern setting; e.g. Lady Derby in a supermarket, Fangs in a doctor's waiting-room, Sir Jasper at a school disco.

◉ Discuss why films, books, and plays which depict the conflict between good and evil are universally appealing. Can you think of any examples of such conflict—and who usually wins?

Topics for written work

◉ Design some period costumes for two of the actors or actresses in A FATE WORSE THAN DEATH.

◉ 'A villain is always more attractive to act, or watch, than a hero.' Discuss.

◉ Write a humorous short story on *one* of the following:
      Lady Derby in a supermarket
      Fangs in a dentist's waiting-room
      Sir Jasper at your school disco.

◉ What background music would you use for a production of A FATE WORSE THAN DEATH? Give some examples and relate them to specific incidents in the play.

Outline 18   Job Lot

Preliminary exercises

Portray the behaviour of people in situations where it is important to be cheerful and polite; e.g. serving in a shop or restaurant, meeting your boy- or girl-friend's parents for the first time, talking to your Headmaster or employer.

Discuss how one behaves at interviews and consider the sort of qualities interviewers look for in a good candidate.

Characterisation

Mr/Miss Matthews
Friendly, helpful and charming.

Mr/Mrs Leach
Fierce and aggressive.

Tom Bowles
Quiet, studious; educated at a Comprehensive School and obtained two O-levels and three CSEs (choose your subjects). School librarian, secretary of the chess club, member of school tennis team. Your hobbies are fishing and photography. Add further details as you wish.

Jean Hughes
Talkative, attractive and friendly; educated at Grammar School and obtained four O-levels (choose your subjects). Prefect and vice-captain of the hockey team. Your interests include the cinema, drawing, and country and western music. Enlarge on these.

Alice Smythe
Well-spoken, ambitious, smart; educated at Public School and obtained three O-levels. Your interests include drama, jazz and foreign travel. Enlarge on these details.

Your play

Mr/Miss Matthews the personnel officer
Mr/Mrs Leach the manager
Tom Bowles ⎫
Jean Hughes ⎬ the three candidates
Alice Smythe ⎭

Scene   office interior

The plot is simple, but the situation is probable—and it could well happen to you soon!

1. Three candidates, Tom, Jean and Alice, have applied for the vacancy for a junior office clerk at an advertising agency. The job has excellent prospects.

2. Seated behind the desk are the two interviewers, Mr Leach and Mr Matthews (or Miss Matthews and Mrs Leach if girls take these parts). In front of the desk is a chair for the candidate who is being interviewed.

3. *The candidates enter* as they are called in by Mr Leach and are interviewed *in turn. They* then *exit* to wait outside.

4. The interviewers, having prepared questions beforehand, talk to the candidates and jot down notes and ideas for later use.

5. Mr Matthews and Mr Leach give their assessment of each candidate's interview before they state who has been selected and the reasons for their choice . . .

Who will be the lucky candidate?

Particular points to rehearse

a   **Interviewers**—thoroughly work out details of the job advertised and details of the company as candidates may well question you about these.
Candidates—consider *why* you want this job, you will probably be asked!

b   Although this is an interesting exercise for the participants it is also a performance of a play which the audience will be watching. So do not let the action drag. Ensure that the interviewers are fully briefed about each candidate and have prepared most of their questions during rehearsal.

c   All actors must ensure that they maintain the role of their characters throughout the play. It is their character who is being interviewed for the job—not themselves.

Matthews
Put candidates at their ease and prepare all relevant details during rehearsal.

Leach
Your function is to try and catch out the candidates with some awkward questions—not a very pleasant person!

Tom, Jean and Alice
Prepare your character well and maintain it throughout the performance.
Elaborate on the details provided, think about your home background, your reasons for wanting the job, your hopes and ambitions. Think of questions you may wish to ask about the company and the job.

EVERYONE
Remember to keep things moving. Don't let the play drag and your audience become bored.

Topics for discussion after a group's performance

● Was this a useful exercise in that the group learned something about interviews? How well did they feel they were interviewed? Were they given the opportunity to give of their best?

● Was this a useful exercise as a piece of drama in that it revealed character, relationships, had some kind of plot, and maintained interest throughout? If not, how might it have been improved?

● Discuss the process of interviewing. Was the interview presented by the group what you would expect from real life? Talk about letters of application, curriculum vitae and references.

● Consider other improvisations about interviews: television interviews, questionnaires, street interviews by a news reporter, in-depth interviews.

● Suggest further improvisations where the three candidates are shown in a more relaxed situation, perhaps involved in one of their hobbies. Does this insight add anything more to their characters which was not brought out during the formal interview?

● Work out an improvisation where Matthews and Leach are asked questions; e.g. in a television studio discussing some trade union dispute, or aspects of advertising methods.

Topics for written work

● Select one group's performance of JOB LOT and state, with reasons, which person you would have chosen for the job.

● Write a piece of dialogue between an interfering newspaper reporter and a busy executive.

● Write the letter you would use to apply for a job in your locality.

● From your experience of watching other groups perform JOB LOT, discuss whether a piece of drama needs to be entertaining as well as informative.

Outline 19 The Three Ages Of Man

Preliminary exercises

Bearing in mind the characteristics of old people (hunched shoulders, stiff joints, creaky voice), mime an elderly person walking, talking, moving, and so forth.

Bearing in mind the characteristics of infants (babyish voice, waddling legs, swaying head, thumb-sucking, etc.), mime a toddler moving and talking.

Characterisation

These outlines are kept deliberately brief as you may wish to prepare your own character's personality. Do work out a full background to the life of each character.

Steven
Jovial, good-natured.

Bob
Energetic.

Philip
Quiet and reserved.

Rachel
Cheerful and intelligent.

Jane
Moody.

Your play

Steven
Bob
Philip　　　　　five friends
Rachel
Jane

Scene　a park

These three scenes, each set in a park, show five friends meeting, playing together and growing up. In the first scene the friends are very young; in the second scene they are aged in their early twenties; and in the final scene they are approaching old age.

A vital point to emphasise is the inter-relationships between characters.

Scene One
The five toddlers, Steven, Bob, Philip, Rachel and Jane, skip into the park and start to play some children's games. Bored with the game, Rachel and Jane begin to quarrel over some silly matter as Philip tries to break up a fight which has developed between Steven and Bob. This scene closes in tears with the children toddling off to their mothers!

Scene Two
Twenty years later. The same characters, now young adults, stroll into the park. Steven enters with his wife, Rachel, and Philip enters with his fiancée, Jane. Bob enters from the other side. They greet each other like long lost friends and tell each other how they are enjoying their work, university or domestic life. (Consequently you must carefully prepare the background to each character for this scene.)
For some reason the two women start to quarrel (what about?). Bob takes Jane's part in the argument and mildly flirts with her.
Eventually the quarrel is amicably settled (how?) and they all depart for a drink.

Scene Three
Another forty-five years have passed. The old folk, Steven and Rachel, and Jane and Bob (who married her after she and Philip broke off their engagement many years ago), enter and talk about their lives and about their old friend, Philip, who emigrated. (Prepare these details carefully.)
When talking about their families a little toddler (played by the actor who took Philip's part) skips in, runs to Rachel, and shouts 'Grandma!' And on this happy note your play ends.

Particular points to rehearse

a All actors must thoroughly prepare the background to their life stories and think about their relationships with the other characters.

b Discuss what are the key points to be conveyed to the audience in the story.

c Vary the action, particularly the entrances and exits for each of the three scenes.

Scene One
Consider how you will portray the antics of the young children, the games played and the way they talk to one another.
Prepare the childish squabble between Rachel and Jane, also the scrap between Steven and Bob.
Rehearse the tearful departure of the toddlers.

Scene Two
Think how you will quickly convey to the audience that this is the same scene, but twenty years later. Also establish the relationships between characters (Steven married to Rachel, Jane engaged to Philip).
Fully convey each character's background when he or she tells us about jobs, ambitions, holidays, family life, etc.
Rehearse the slight quarrel between Jane and Rachel. How did the quarrel start and how will it end?
Prepare Bob's mild flirtation with Jane and her response. She is engaged, at present, to Philip but will eventually marry Bob. How does Philip react and how will this scene end?

Scene Three
Clearly depict the old age of the characters and, as in scene two, further details of their lives; e.g. retirement, Jane married to Bob, etc.
Convey the details of Philip's emigration and any news about him. (Why do you think he emigrated?)
Prepare the cue for the entry of the grandchild.

Topics for discussion after a group's performance

● How successfully did the actors portray their different ages? Did the basic character of each remain consistent? How thoroughly was the background to each character portrayed? Was there too much detail? Did the relevant key points come across clearly?

● How convincing were the inter-relationships between characters?

● How dramatically significant was the entry of the grandchild at the end of the play? How varied was the action of the improvisation? Did one scene tend to have the same pace as another or was there sufficient variety and contrast?

● There are many improvisations which one might suggest about the dramatic moments in each of the characters' lives; e.g. Philip's decision to leave the country, Bob's courtship of Jane. What others can the class suggest?

● Work out an improvisation where you portray your own lives in twenty years time.

● Discuss books, programmes and films which deal with different aspects of life as one grows up.

Topics for written work

● Select one of the characters from the play and write a section from his or her biography.

● Design a poster inviting people to watch a performance of THE THREE AGES OF MAN. What informative details should such a poster include?

● Write two character studies: one of someone in your class as they are today, and a second in which you describe what he or she will be like in twenty years time.

● Take any character from THE THREE AGES OF MAN and draw a design for his or her face, using theatrical make-up, to make the character appear very old. Include explanatory notes.

Outline 20   Both Sides Of The Coin

Preliminary exercises

Start an argument about some trivial matter; e.g. whose turn to wash the dishes, which cinema to go to, whether to spend money on a new item of clothing. Then ask the people involved in the argument to present their points of view to the audience. Re-run the scene with a bias towards one point of view.

Discuss how you might depict the interior of a vehicle; e.g. a car, bus, train, aeroplane, tank.

Characterisation

You will notice from the outline of the play that the characters are presented in two contrasting ways. Study these.

Mrs Hyde
A Kind-hearted old lady.
B Irritable old hag.

Sam
A Fierce and impatient.
B Jovial and friendly.

P.C. Higgins
A & B Impartial and efficient.

Passengers
A Sympathetic towards the old lady.
B Critical of the old woman.

Your play

Mrs Hyde   an elderly lady
Sam   the bus-conductor
First Passenger
Second Passenger
P.C. Higgins

Scene   inside a bus

There are different points of view to everything. What follows is an improvisation of the same scene from two points of view . . .

A   **As Mrs Hyde sees it—**

1 The irritable bus conductor collects fares from two passengers as Mrs Hyde struggles into the bus. The First Passenger rises to give her the seat and she politely thanks him and sits.

2 The conductor rudely demands the fare. It is more than Mrs Hyde usually pays and she politely points out his error. The conductor curtly demands the extra money and Mrs Hyde politely refuses to pay.

3 Angrily, the conductor hurls abuse at Mrs Hyde and finally refuses to move the bus until she pays or gets off the bus. The other two passengers join in the argument, taking Mrs Hyde's side and condemning the conductor.

4 *P.C. Higgins enters* to sort out the matter and takes a statement from Mrs Hyde in which she expresses her point of view.

B   **As the conductor sees it—**

1 *Mrs Hyde enters* as the friendly conductor collects fares from the two passengers and exchanges jokes with them. Irritably, the elderly Mrs Hyde demands a seat and the First Passenger reluctantly vacates his/her seat.

2 Snappily, Mrs Hyde presents her fare. It is not enough and the conductor politely asks for the correct amount, but she refuses and argues.

3 The conductor declares that it would be unfair to move the bus until she has paid or decided to find another means of travel. The other two passengers join in the argument, supporting the conductor's point of view.

4 *P.C. Higgins enters* to sort out the matter and takes a statement from the conductor in which he gives his version of the incident.

Particular points to rehearse

a Clearly emphasise the contrast between the two episodes, ensuring that the actors completely reverse their roles.

b Rehearse the arguments, both expressed from different points of view, building up to a noisy and heated argument. Prepare a cue for the policeman's entry.

c Consider how the scenes will end with the policeman resolving the situation.

Mrs Hyde
Convey your confusion over the fares. Rehearse the arguments in which you become involved, clearly portraying the different aspects of your character.

Sam
Strongly portray your different character in the two scenes and rehearse your arguments with Mrs Hyde.

P.C. Higgins
Prepare the cue for your dramatic entry at the height of the quarrel and consider how you will resolve the situation.

Passengers
Consider your different attitudes in each scene. Rehearse your gradual involvement in the arguments.

Finally, when the play is over, remain on stage and ask the audience to question you about your different attitudes.

Topics for discussion after a group's performance

● Invite the actors to remain on stage and let the audience ask them questions about their different attitudes in the play. How was the emphasis shifted to support a different viewpoint?

● How useful was this technique of demonstrating characterisation from different points of view? Suggest further improvisations using this technique; e.g. political differences, racial questions, advertising.

● Comment on the way in which the quarrel developed and picked up pace.

Topics for written work

● Write a brief account of an argument between a teacher and a pupil, from both points of view.

● Write the dialogue of a quarrel between a politician and an unemployed worker.

● Design two stage sets for BOTH SIDES OF THE COIN—one set for theatre-in-the-round, and one for a stage behind the proscenium arch.

Supplementary exercises

The following ideas may be useful for odd minutes after a performance or for revision.

1 Mime a person moving through different kinds of weather conditions; e.g. blizzard, gale, sandstorm, heavy rain, fog, icy wind.

2 Mime the actions of someone climbing up a tree, ladder, rope, drainpipe. What other mimes of upward movement can you devise?

3 Imagine that you have been frozen inside a solid block of ice. Slowly, as it thaws, you come back to life.

4 Mime someone playing a sport; e.g. table tennis, hockey, throwing the discus. Suddenly at a given signal you 'freeze' and stand motionless.

5 Mime the actions of someone trying to keep his/her balance; e.g. walking a tightrope, erecting a television aerial on a roof, edging along a cliff-face.

6 You are trapped in a lift, or locked in a small shed, or shut in a cell. Mime your attempts to escape from such an enclosed environment.

7 Perform a delicate task such as repairing a watch, making a model aircraft, painting, embroidering. Mime the skilful and careful movements involved.

8 Perform a strenuous task such as cutting down a tree, moving a heavy piece of furniture, using a pickaxe. Depict the strong and muscular movements involved.

9 Mime the cautious actions of a person entering an unknown scene such as a haunted room, an eerie crypt, a dark cellar, a graveyard.

10 Perform an everyday task such as drinking coffee, doing your homework, washing the dishes. Suddenly you are struck by an invisible force! Show what happens.

11 Demonstrate reaction to a sudden shock. Suppose a scientist mixes chemicals which suddenly explode, or an electrician repairing a television set receives a violent electric shock . . . What other incidents can you think of?

12 Mime the actions of someone performing a skilled occupation; e.g. a dentist, piano tuner, potter making a vase, surgeon. See whether the class recognises what it is you are doing.

13 You are in a foreign country and have to purchase some items from a shop. As you cannot speak the language you must mime your requirements. Your shopping list might contain a sliced loaf, an egg whisk, and some cough medicine. What other items can you mime successfully?

14 Portray the reaction of different 'types' to a simple incident. Suppose a young lady drops her handkerchief. It is picked up and returned with varying degrees of charm. Who might simply ignore it?

15 Portray the characteristic behaviour of different character 'types'; e.g. a vicar, a poet, an all-in wrestler, a pop star. Devise a simple setting for your character, such as in a café, opening a bazaar, or buying a car. See whether the class can guess what type of character you are.

16 Convey the behaviour and facial expressions of someone undergoing a rapid change of emotions. Suppose you've won the pools/you've not posted the coupon; you buy a new motor bike/you crash it; you admire a china ornament/you drop it.

17 Imagine that you are at a zoo, a circus or a football match. Show from your reactions and your facial expressions what it is you are watching.

18 Mime someone climbing down into a hole, or descending a rope, or walking downstairs. Try to devise some other situations which portray a strong downward movement. (Why is it more difficult to portray a downward movement than an upward movement?)

19 Pretend that you are talking to an imaginary person. Mime the conversation as it moves from friendly greeting, through some sort of disagreement, to angry quarrel. Think of a particular situation such as talking to a neighbour, meeting an old friend, scolding a child, arguing with a door-to-door salesman.

20 Mime the actions of a person falling asleep, turning over restlessly, sleep-walking and waking up feeling startled.

21 Mime the actions of someone putting on an unusual form of clothing; e.g. a diving-suit, an astronaut's space suit, a suit of armour, an expensive gown or wedding dress, a clown's outfit. Try to convey the quality and texture of the clothes.

22 Present a mime of a postman delivering cumbersome parcels and letters.

23 Ask someone to write down an adverb ('joyfully', 'gloomily', and so forth). Then perform a simple task in such a way that the rest of the class can recognise what the word is.

24 Perform the behaviour and actions of a very young child going for a walk in the park, eating a sweet, and feeding the ducks. Then repeat the scene, this time conveying the movements of a very old person.

25 Improvise a short scene where your character intrudes into a place where he, or she, should not be. You could depict a drunk in a library, a lost child wandering into the teachers' staff-room, a man going by mistake to a ladies' coffee morning. What other incidents can you think of? You could use two or three actors for this exercise.

26 Portray someone making a rather confused telephone call. You have phoned a large department store asking for someone to repair your leaking washing machine. Unfortunately you keep being put through to the wrong departments and you speak at cross-purposes to unhelpful assistants. Try to portray the confusion.

27 Two of you devise a sequence where you speak to each other in such strong dialects that neither can understand the other. (You could make up a strange, unintelligible dialect if you wish.)

28 The whole class combines to form an organic unity. You depict a living creature such as a dragon, a crocodile, a microbe, and so forth.

29 A small group adopts a word—'sponge'—as its sole means of communication. You recite it with different accents, moods and intonations to convey the sense of what you are expressing. You then portray a short scene: men in a pub discussing the weather, women in a shop gossiping about the price of food, a school teacher scolding a naughty pupil.

30 The class forms a choral orchestra where different units recite the appropriate sound in the manner of concrete poetry. You could represent a busy street scene, an orchestra, a war requiem, a pop group. Finally you might select a suitable poem and perform some choral speaking.